The Chapel Veil

Elizabeth Black and Emily Sparks

The Chapel Veil

The Symbol of the Spouse of Christ

SOPHIA INSTITUTE PRESS
Manchester, New Hampshire

First published by Requiem Press in 2005
and Roman Catholic Books: Fort Collins, CO, in 2010.

Cover by Updatefordesign Studio.

Cover image: Lace Veil by Tom Pumford on Unsplash.

Sophia Institute Press
Box 5284, Manchester, NH 03108
1-800-888-9344

www.SophiaInstitute.com

paperback ISBN 978-1-64413-906-6

ebook ISBN 978-1-64413-907-3

Library of Congress Control Number: 2022951765

2nd printing

Contents

Preface. 3

The Veil as a Symbol of the Identity
and Vocation of a Woman. 11

The Veil and the Eucharist. 21

Acknowledgments 33

About the Authors. .37

The Chapel Veil

Preface

In the matter of reforming things, as distinct from deforming them, there is one plain and simple principle; a principle which will probably be called a paradox. There exists in such a case a certain institution or law; let us say, for the sake of simplicity, a fence or gate erected across a road. The more modern type of reformer goes gaily up to it and says, "I don't see the use of this; let us clear it away." To which the more intelligent type of reformer will do well to answer: "If you don't see the use of it, I certainly won't let you clear it away. Go away and think. Then, when you can come back and tell me that you do see the use of it, I may allow you to destroy it."

—G.K. Chesterton

THE CHAPEL VEIL has been the victim of the "more modern type of reformer" Chesterton refers to in the epigraph. It was easy to discard because not many knew its purpose, the tradition of its theology, or its symbolism. Many *thought* they knew the symbolism of the chapel veil—simply a symbol of male domination—yet they were and are still gravely mistaken.

We do not always have to understand why we must follow this command or that tradition—love demands obedience regardless of understanding. And, in fact, the Faith is full of mysteries we will never fully comprehend. Yet we should always strive for greater understanding.

When we do make the effort to extend our understanding of the mysteries of the Faith and the traditions and doctrines, our prayer life and our relationship with our Lord is deepened.

This little volume contains two short essays, similar in scope and in perception. These essays enlighten an area that has been dark for too long. The Church has always exalted the role of women — yet the Modernists would have you believe the opposite and use the chapel veil as an example in their deception.

Yet women who truly desire to embrace their vocation and deepen their devotion to the Holy Eucharist should read the following pages carefully. These short pieces contain the reasons, rooted in Scripture and in the writings of the Church Fathers, why two young women wear the chapel veil. Their discoveries concerning the theology, symbolism, and tradition of the veil may enlighten you — not only about the veil, but about marriage, men, women, the Eucharist, and Heaven. Again, the ideas herein are not new, but have simply been forgotten.

Oremus pro invicem!—Let us pray for each other.

J. Curley, Bethune, SC

The Veil as a Symbol of the Identity and Vocation of a Woman

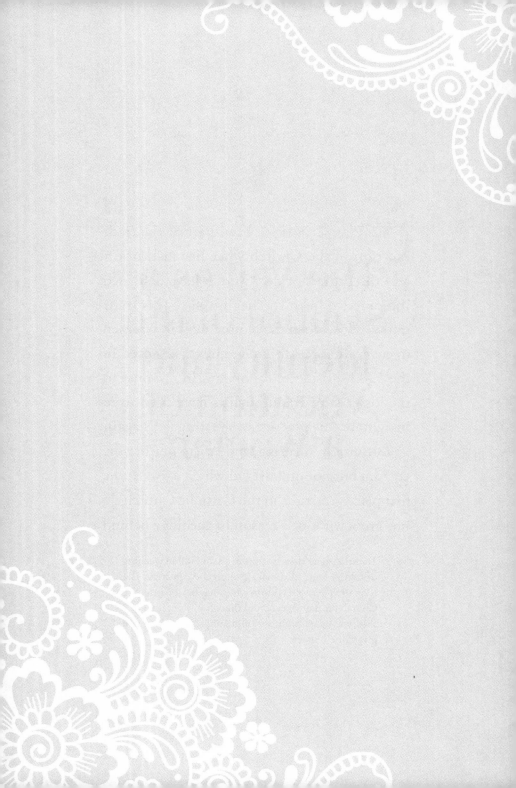

✠

CHAPEL VEILS HAVE been part of the tradition of the Church since her institution, and the Fathers of the Church have defended the practice from the beginning.[1] This tradition was lost when the requirement for women to cover their heads in church was removed in the 1983 revision of canon law. In response to the loss, many Traditionalists have tried to reinvigorate this practice by wearing veils again. Unfortunately, there is a tendency to practice the custom but not understand why it exists in the first place. Practices in the Catholic Church do not grow without a reason or theology behind

1 Tradition here does not mean the infallible teaching of Christ handed down through the Apostles. The term used here is a custom which has been part of the Church for many years, and though it is not infallible, this type of tradition is honored by the Church and given due respect.

them. The tradition of chapel veils has also been viewed with misunderstanding and mistrust by non-Traditionalists because it seems unnecessary and outdated. Thus, it is important for both Traditionalists and non-Traditionalists to understand the theological meaning and symbolism behind the Church's custom of chapel veils. The theology of the chapel veil is rooted in woman's identity and her relationship with man and Christ and symbolic of the unchanging role of woman in creation.

These explanations are primarily the fruit of discussions with friends and so are open to development. My arguments will be from a purely theological or symbolic aspect. Thus, I will not address the psychological or social reasons for wearing a veil, which are often dealt with by other writers. Although social and psychological explanations have value, they are of less weight and import than those based on theology.

St. John Chrysostom develops the theology of the veil in a beautiful way. He draws a comparison between the relationship of man and woman to Christ and woman. Woman, because she was created by being drawn from man's side, is constantly trying to return to him. She desires the original unity of one flesh and one bone. This is evident in her desire for intimacy and love. This tendency back to her source is beautifully expressed in the marital act, where once more woman physically becomes one with man, flesh and bone. The desire for unity between man and woman is a mirror of the relationship of Christ and the soul. Christ loves man so much that not only did He die on the Cross, but He expresses His love by becoming physically present in the Divine Eucharist. He is the Divine Lover of the soul, and He becomes the

Spouse of the woman, the bride. As woman longs for union with man in human relationships, so she is constantly drawn to unity with God. He calls her to become one with Him: to come under His side and become flesh of His flesh and bone of His bone. This occurs during the reception of Holy Eucharist, which is the consummation of the union between Christ and the soul. The covering of the head with a veil symbolizes the reality of woman sheltered in the side of her Source and becoming one with Him. She becomes covered and hidden in her Divine Spouse. The veil is a symbol of the relationship of woman's soul to Christ.

In addition, the veil represents woman's position in the hierarchy of God's order. Man is the protector of woman, while woman is the protected. Because of their respective identities, men and women show reverence to their Creator in different ways. For the man, uncovering his head is a sign of respect and submission to his superior. This is exemplified beautifully in the Traditional Mass when the priest enters wearing a biretta and uncovers his head before beginning the worship of God. This respect for hierarchy is shown differently by women. Rather than baring the head, women cover the head to show respect and submission to authority. Thus, to don a veil for Mass represents woman's submission to God. She acknowledges her role in God's creation.

The veil also is a physical sign of woman's role as a tabernacle. The tabernacle contains Christ, the True Life, within it. Similarly, woman was created with the privilege of being a vessel of life—literally capable of bearing life within her. In this way, she is a kind of living tabernacle. The Holy Tabernacle is sacred because it contains Life Itself, and likewise, woman is sacred because she protects life within her. The Holy

Tabernacle is so holy that it is veiled to preserve its purity and holiness. Woman wears a veil to cover her sacredness as a temple of life. This veiling of the Tabernacle and the woman is also a visible reminder to the faithful that these vessels have a special role. Woman, then, like the Tabernacle, should be physically veiled.

Finally, the veil symbolizes woman as the "sealed garden" (Song of Sol. 4:12) whose fruits are reserved for God. The Song of Songs uses this analogy when speaking of the relationship of Christ and the soul. The Divine Lover says of his beloved, "A garden locked is my sister, my bride"; and the beloved responds, "Let my beloved come to his garden, and eat its choicest fruits" (Song of Sol. 4:12, 16). Woman's soul is a garden which, when cultivated, yields much fruit. But it is also a sealed garden because she opens it only to God, particularly in the union of Holy Communion. It is her special gift to her

God. The veil, then, symbolizes this sheltered, sealed garden, which is preserved and tilled for the Divine Lover. It is a physical sign that God is formally being sought and worshipped. It symbolizes preservation of self for a complete self-giving to another.[2]

The custom, then, of women covering their heads is not meaningless or outdated, but has theological symbolism and importance for the modern era. By covering her head, woman acknowledges submission to Christ her spouse, the sacrifice of her glory, and adoration and humility before God. Although it is not a sin to remain bareheaded, the veil has such beautiful symbolism that it is a praiseworthy and important way to give glory to God.

[2] This is an essential reason that religious wear permanent veils, for they are the vowed spouses of God, and they preserve the garden of their soul for Him alone in a unique way.

The Veil and the Eucharist

✠

WHY THE VEIL? That is a question that many Catholics ask, especially through the past century. The chapel veil has been practically eradicated in this age; it is often remembered as just another one of those man-made symbols to show the superiority of men. This explanation is inaccurate, for the meaning of the veil goes much deeper. It is a sign that penetrates the Mystery of Faith, the Eucharist, and is also a symbol of the privilege of the feminine vocation. It is important and necessary to bring back the custom of veils in church.

The reason for the loss of the tradition of women wearing head coverings in church is often misunderstood. It was not a result of Vatican II—there is no mention of veils in the documents of that council. Nor was it completely a result of the removal of their mandate from the 1983 revision of canon law. This is evident because even before Vatican II it became more and more unusual to see women wearing veils in church. The tradition was replaced by a fashionable hat in order to keep the letter of the law.

The primary reason for the veil is that it is a symbol of the Eucharist as the consummation of Christ's love for His Church. In the beginning, woman was created from the side of man. St. John Chrysostom compares this creation and the creation of the Church — he says that as Eve was brought forth from Adam's side, so the Church was brought into being from Christ's pierced side on the Cross. If one applies this principle to the male and female person, it is seen that it is man's call to symbolize Christ and imitate Christ's love for the Church in his love for his wife; and woman's call to symbolize the Church and to love her husband with the love the Church has for Jesus Christ, as St. Paul teaches in Ephesians 5. There is an innate longing in man and woman to return to the original unity, to become one flesh once again, which is realized through the sacrament of marriage. The love the Church and Christ share is spousal, and as the conjugal act is the consummation of an earthly marriage, the Eucharist is the consummation of the heavenly marriage. In the conjugal act the two earthly spouses become one flesh, and original unity is regained. In the conjugal act the woman is literally brought back under the arm of her husband. In the Eucharist the Church becomes one flesh with Christ and is brought back under the outstretched arm of Christ Crucified. The veiled woman and the unveiled man represent the essence of this mystery. Since it is seen in Ephesians that a man is called to become like Christ by assuming the duty and responsibility of headship, in the presence of the Eucharist man must uncover his head. When he receives the Eucharist he becomes transformed into the image of Christ, and this especially includes partaking in Christ's leadership (see 1 Cor. 11). The woman's role is different, but no less important. It is through the Eucharist that the Church becomes Christ's body, and returns to His side to be one flesh. A veil on a woman is a sign of this mystery—she, as a living symbol of the Church, covers her head to show that she has become one with Christ, and that He is her head. She is truly, physically, under the arm of Christ. The veil shows that for women holiness is attained *not* by partaking in the headship of Christ, but by loving Him as a spouse and receiving Him. Because of this order of headship and receptive love, the veil does show woman's submission to man, but that is a secondary meaning to the primary meaning, which is Eucharistic.

One objection I have heard frequently made by those who see the veil as only a sign of earthly submission to men is this: Why does a woman only cover her head in church? Should she not cover it all the time? Her submissive role does not begin and end in the building of a church. The answer to this is much easier to understand once one sees the Eucharistic meaning. Since the veil is a sign of the Eucharistic Presence, it is in the church building, in God's house, and in the presence of His Body, Blood, Soul, and Divinity, that a woman's head should be covered, for reasons stated above. The only exceptions are consecrated women. It is no accident nuns should have their heads covered all the time. Because of their perpetual vows, they are constantly a symbol of the spousal relationship of the Church to Christ. Christ is always and will always be their husband, even on earth, so their heads are covered as a reminder of this reality.

There is also a distinctly Marian symbol to the veil. Women are meant to imitate Mary, the ideal woman and perfect human being, in a special way. Mary is always veiled in her apparitions and images, and was throughout her life on earth. This is because Mary is the holiest of human persons—she is holy in the sense that she was perfectly good, and also she is holy in the sense that she is completely set apart from the rest of creation. Throughout salvation history, holy things were veiled in order to preserve their proper mystery and to show that they are set apart. Notable examples of this in the Old Testament are the Holy of Holies in the Temple—which was veiled by a curtain, and Mount Sinai—which was veiled by clouds when the glory of God came upon it. The glory of God not only rested upon Mary, but dwelt within

Mary. Thus the splendour of the tabernacle of her body was veiled. This sheds new light on 1 Cor. 11:10: "For this reason a woman ought to have a symbol of authority on her head, because of the angels." "Because of the angels" is a mysterious statement. It has been suggested that the angels referred to are the angels atop the Ark of the Covenant, because their heads were covered with their wings. It is upon the angels that the glory of the Lord would rest when He came upon the Ark and dwelt with His Chosen People. He "overshadowed" the Ark in the same way He "overshadowed" Mary, the spouse of the Holy Spirit. It is a woman's privilege to wear a veil before God as an outward sign of this honor given to the Woman.

Furthermore, as Dr. Alice von Hildebrand teaches in her book *The Privilege of Being a Woman*, every woman is holy—in the meaning of being set apart because of what her body is designed to do. The creation of a new person requires both a man and a woman, but it is within the woman's body that this new life is conceived. At conception, a soul is directly infused into this new person, and this infusion is an act of God. God touches a woman's body in a way He does not touch man's. The veil is a sign of this awesome vocation of women, and of the holiness of her body.

Women are privileged to veil themselves in the presence of God because of the veil's Eucharistic symbolism and of the honor for women to be the personification of the glorious Bride of Christ — the Church. Furthermore, it is a sign of the call to imitate the Mother of God and a reminder of the holiness of the body of a woman. The presence of a veil shows forth not only the glory of woman, but also the glory of man and his vocation to headship — it shows the God-given complementarity of the sexes. Veils are not just a man-made token of female inferiority, nor are they a way to show off that one is a "Traditionalist." When they are worn for either of those reasons, they are entirely shriven of the supernatural meaning. It is this loss of the sense of the supernatural that robbed many churches of this custom. Since it has been demonstrated that the woman's veil is a powerful symbol of Christ's Presence in the Eucharist, the renewal of this tradition will help to bring about reverence for the amazing gift of the Eucharist, which has been lost.

Acknowledgments

OUR THANKS TO St. Paul the Apostle; St. John Chrysostom (especially homilies on Ephesians and Corinthians); St. Bede; St. Ambrose; canon law; John Paul II; Drs. Dietrich and Alice von Hildebrand; Sabatino Carnazzo, and hence most likely St. Ephrem and other Eastern Fathers, and any author commenting on the Edenic paradigm; Sr. Katherine Michelle, O.P.; Professor Jenislawski of Christendom College; and the ladies of St. Catherine's Hall, Christendom College.

About the Authors

✠

ELIZABETH BLACK GRADUATED with a degree in classics from Christendom College in 2007 and has since dedicated herself to sacred music as organist and choir director in the Boston and Washington areas. After working for two years at Thomas More College, she moved to Northern Virginia where she is currently a full-time choir teacher and professional singer.

EMILY SPARKS GREW up in Hilton Head Island, South Carolina, and graduated from Christendom College in 2007. She now lives in Front Royal, Virginia, with her husband and children.

Sophia Institute

Sophia Institute is a nonprofit institution that seeks to nurture the spiritual, moral, and cultural life of souls and to spread the Gospel of Christ in conformity with the authentic teachings of the Roman Catholic Church.

Sophia Institute Press fulfills this mission by offering translations, reprints, and new publications that afford readers a rich source of the enduring wisdom of mankind.

Sophia Institute also operates the popular online Catholic resource CatholicExchange.com. *Catholic Exchange* provides world news from a Catholic perspective as well as daily devotionals and articles that will help readers to grow in holiness and live a life consistent with the teachings of the Church.

In 2013, Sophia Institute launched Sophia Institute for Teachers to renew and rebuild Catholic culture through service to Catholic education. With the goal of nurturing the spiritual, moral, and cultural life of souls, and an abiding respect for the role and work of teachers, we strive to provide materials and programs that are at once enlightening to the mind and ennobling to the heart; faithful and complete, as well as useful and practical.

Sophia Institute gratefully recognizes the Solidarity Association for preserving and encouraging the growth of our apostolate over the course of many years. Without their generous and timely support, this book would not be in your hands.

www.SophiaInstitute.com
www.CatholicExchange.com
www.SophiaInstituteforTeachers.org

Sophia Institute Press® is a registered trademark of Sophia Institute.
Sophia Institute is a tax-exempt institution as defined by the
Internal Revenue Code, Section 501(c)(3). Tax I.D. 22-2548708.